A **start me up** Book

The Universe

To the Limits of Space and Time

By Dr. Erich Uebelacker

Illustrated by Manfred Kostka and Joachim Knappe

Hubble Space Telescope

Tessloff Publishing

Preface

Even in ancient times, most cultures tried to understand and explain the cosmos or universe — they often called it simply "the world." Usually they believed the Earth was the center of the universe. Surrounding the universe was an outer shell to which the constellations of stars were attached, and beyond this lay the realm of the gods. It has only been about 500 years now since Copernicus demonstrated that the Sun is at the center of our solar system, not the Earth. Scientists later recognized that our Sun isn't even the only one — it is surrounded by millions of suns. All of these solar systems, ours included, make up our galaxy — the Milky Way.

Thanks to powerful telescopes and space probes, we now know that even our galaxy is not the only one. The universe contains billions of other galaxies, and they form huge groups called superclusters. The universe has not always existed, however. It was probably created by the "big bang," about 15 billion years ago. Space, time, and matter all began with the "big bang."

Every day we receive new data and photographs from the far reaches of space. Hubble Space Telescope has given us incomparably beautiful and valuable images from the farthest reaches of the universe. As new information comes in, old theories, ideas, and explanations are sometimes disproved and must be replaced. At the frontiers of science this is nothing unusual — it is the norm.

The science that studies the structure and evolution of the universe is called cosmology. This **start me up!**™ book introduces readers to modern cosmology. It discusses questions about the beginning and end of the universe, about space and time, and also about the shape and boundaries of the universe.

Volume 7

PUBLISHERS: Tessloff Publishing, Quadrillion Media LLC

EDITOR: Alan Swensen

PICTURE SOURCES: Astrofoto, Leichlingen: pp. 1 Shigemi Numazawa, 3 NASA, 4/5 Koch, 6 ESO, 9 NASA (2), 10/11 NASA, 12, 15 Koch, 16 Shigemi Numazawa, 17 NASA, 19 NASA (2), 19 Shigemi Numazawa, 20 Shigemi Numazawa, 21 Koch, 22 NASA, 22 ZEISS, 22 NASA, 24 Shigemi Numazawa, 28 NOAO, 28 NASA, 29 ROE/AAT Board, 30 NASA, 34/35 APB, 36 Koch, 39 NOAO, 39 Hale Observatorium, 41 NASA, 44 NASA, 45 Shigemi Numazawa, 46 NASA. Bildagentur Schuster, Oberursel: p. 46. Bildarchiv Preussischer Kulturbesitz, Berlin: p. 36. Planetarium Hamburg: pp. 5, 6, 6 ESO, 9 Hansen Planetarium/Salt Lake City, 12, 14 (3), 20, 22 NASA, 44 NASA, 45, 46 NASA.

COVER PHOTOS: Astrofoto, Leichlingen

ILLUSTRATIONS: Manfred Kostka and Joachim Knappe

Translated by Richard Quinn and Anja Peschel

COPYRIGHT: © MCMXCVIII Tessloff Publishing, Burgschmietstrasse 2-4, 90419 Nuremberg, Germany
© MCMXCVIII Quadrillion Media LLC, 10105 East Via Linda Road, Suite 103-390, Scottsdale AZ 85258, USA

Visit us on the World Wide Web at http://www.quadrillionusa.com

Library of Congress Cataloging-in-Publication Data is available.

ISBN 1-58185-015-8

Printed in Belgium

Printing 10 9 8 7 6 5 4 3 2 1

Table of Contents

Preface   2

Table of Contents   3

Looking into Space

How do astronomers investigate space?   4

Why do stars shine?   7

How far away are the nearest stars?   8

How are stars created?   9

What happens when a star dies?   11

What are white dwarves and pulsars?   12

What is a black hole?   12

What are star clusters?   14

Where in the universe are we?   15

What is dark matter?   16

Are there other galaxies?   17

What do we know about the distribution of galaxies in space?   18

How fast do galaxies move?   19

A Beginning — and No Ending?

How old is our solar system?   21

Has our galaxy always existed?   22

How did the universe begin?   23

What are the four fundamental forces of nature?   24

What happened at the very beginning of the universe?   25

How were atoms formed?   26

How were the galaxies created?   27

How was our solar system created?   29

Why is there life on Earth?   31

Is there evidence for the big bang?   32

Have space and time always existed?   33

Infinite expansion – or collapse?   33

What will the universe look like in the future?   34

How does God fit into the big bang theory?   35

Elliptic galaxy at the edge of the Coma Berenices cluster — photographed by the Hubble Space Telescope.

Is the Universe Infinite?

How did earlier cultures picture the universe?   36

What was the "Copernican Revolution"?   37

Why does it get dark at night?   37

What was astronomy like at the beginning of the 20th century?   38

Can the universe be finite and still have no boundaries?   39

What is space deformation?   40

Can we see to infinity?   41

Extraterrestrial Life

Is there life on other planets in our solar system?   44

Are there other planetary systems?   45

Are we really alone in space?   46

How can we make contact with extraterrestrials?   46

Why haven't we heard from extraterrestrials?   47

Index   48

Looking into Space

<table>
<tr><td>

How do astronomers investigate space?

</td></tr>
</table>

Already thousands of years ago scholars were studying the universe, the space surrounding the Earth and containing the stars and other heavenly bodies. They tried to explain the structures of these objects and to measure their size.

Modern space research began in the early 17th century. The Italian physicist and astronomer Galileo Galilei was the first person to look at the stars through a telescope. In 1609 Galileo discovered the mountains on our Moon and the moons orbiting the planet Jupiter. In the years that followed, people made bigger and bigger telescopes that showed us millions of distant worlds. To these observers they just looked like little points of light. Much later scientists learned how to split the light from stars and to analyze the resulting light spectra. Lots of information about stars was found out using this method, including information about their temperatures, compositions, magnetic fields, and movements.

Except for a few attempts to collect space radiation with balloons, scientists before 1932 had only studied starlight we can see on Earth. Unfortunately, the atmosphere absorbs most of the radiation coming from space. Lots

TELESCOPES

There are two basic types of telescopes. The refracting telescope, or refractor, uses a lens to collect and focus the light of the stars. The reflecting telescope, or reflector, uses a concave mirror — a concentrating reflector — to collect and focus the light. The larger the mirror, the more light it can collect. The mirrors of big telescopes are several yards in diameter.

Even using a small telescope you can see hundreds of thousands of stars. These points of light are actually stars like our Sun, only much further away.

Observatories, like the European Southern Observatory in Chile shown above, are almost always located high in the mountains. The large telescopes used by astronomers are usually housed in dome-shaped buildings.

The word "PARTICLE" comes from Latin and simply means "small part."

and lots of information from distant galaxies and stars never reaches the observatories where astronomers work. In 1932 scientists began investigating radio waves from deep space. Like light, these waves can penetrate the Earth's atmosphere.

Space travel has overcome all of these barriers. Numerous satellites investigate X-rays and ultraviolet radiation from space. Other satellites measure infrared radiation from newly forming stars and planets. Space probes study Jupiter's atmosphere or use the most modern radar technology to discover volcanoes and craters on Venus. The first astronauts landed on the Moon in 1969. They collected Moon rocks that scientists studied for clues about the age and evolution of our solar system. Specially built satellites examine radiation given off shortly after the universe was created, others investigate particle streams emitted by the Sun or released by the explosion of stars.

Even visible light can be seen more clearly from space than from the Earth's surface. We shouldn't forget that light from distant stars has to pass through the dirty "basement window" of our atmosphere before it reaches our observatories. The Hubble Space Telescope, which has been orbiting the Earth since 1990, has been able to help us overcome these problems. Using the Hubble telescope, astronomers have been able to see newly forming planets and areas surrounding black holes for the very first time. They have also gained better insight into the beginning of the universe.

Astronomers on the Earth have also made tremendous progress in recent years. Gigantic radio tele-

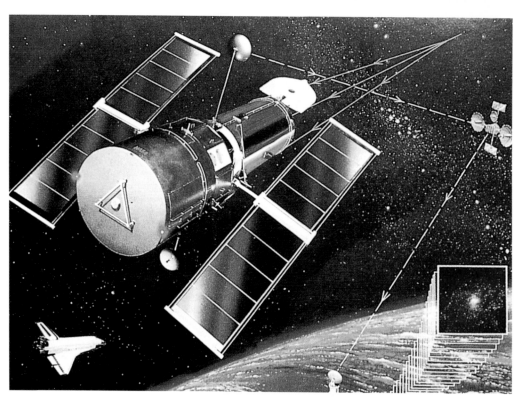

NEUTRINO ASTRONOMY

Neutrinos are tiny, electrically neutral elementary particles. They are produced during nuclear fusion inside the Sun. They can pass right through the Sun, and scientists can learn a lot about the Sun's hot center by examining these neutrinos with sensitive instruments.

From its orbit outside the interference of Earth's atmosphere the Hubble Space Telescope can get a much clearer view of distant objects than an observatory on Earth can. Many of the pictures in this book were taken by this telescope.

scopes and the ultramodern optical equipment on Earth still play a very important role in astronomy. The disadvantages of their position on Earth are overcome by their large size and advanced technology, which help them deal with distortion from the atmosphere. The "Very Large Telescope" in the mountains of Chile has been especially important in setting new standards.

There are even observatories located underground! Here scientists study tiny particles released by the

Sun or by exploding stars. These tiny particles are called neutrinos. Neutrinos can pass through sheets of lead and entire mountain ranges, so scientists study them here where

Astronomers use large telescopes to look far into space and explore galaxies that are millions of light years away.

The "Very Large Telescope" of the European Southern Observatory on top of Cerro Paranal in Chile. It consists of four mirror telescopes, each about 27 feet across.

PARTICLE ACCELERATOR

Astronomers believe the temperature directly after the big bang was extremely high. That means that atomic nuclei and particles moved about at very high speeds. Using a particle accelerator scientists can raise elementary particles and atomic nuclei to speeds similar to those at the beginning of the universe. This simulates conditions at the time of the "big bang."

In the center of the Sun, nuclear fusion combines four hydrogen nuclei to form a single helium nucleus. The helium nucleus has slightly less mass than four hydrogen nuclei. The difference in mass is released as energy.

all other particles are filtered out. Even physicists who work with the huge "particle accelerators" are exploring space in an indirect way. They are able to recreate conditions like the ones that existed shortly after the universe was formed. This research helps astronomers who study the "big bang," the birth of the universe.

On a clear, moonless night it is possible to see about 2,000 stars with the naked eye. Except for planets like Venus or Jupiter, each of these light points is a distant sun. These suns are so far away that they look to us like pinpoints of light in the night sky.

Why do stars shine?

Each of these stars is moving through space at an unimaginable speed. A human lifetime isn't long enough for us to notice their movements because of the huge distance between these stars and us. If you look at the night sky, it looks like some stars fit together to form figures — we call them "constellations." For thousands of years these constellations seem to have remained unchanged.

It is possible to see hundreds of thousands of stars using a good pair of binoculars or a small telescope. Many of these stars are actually much brighter than our own Sun, others send out relatively little light. Stars are big balls of hot gas that are so hot at the center that energy is released in a process called nuclear fusion. During

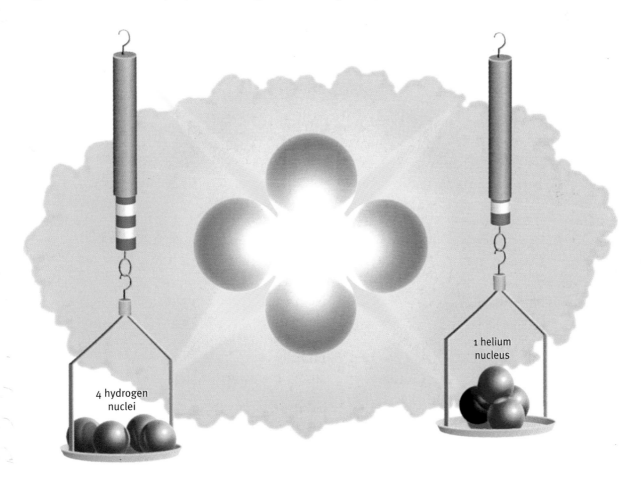

4 hydrogen nuclei

1 helium nucleus

Even if a super spaceship could travel a hundred times faster than today's space probes, it would still take centuries before it reached the nearest stars.

nuclear fusion, the nuclei of small atoms combine to create larger atoms. This process releases tremendous amounts of energy.

In the interior of our Sun — and in billions of other stars — the following process takes place: the nuclei of four tiny hydrogen atoms combine in a complex way to form the nucleus of a helium atom. The nucleus of the helium atom is somewhat lighter than the four hydrogen nuclei it is made from. The mass that is lost gets converted into energy. Stars that have a huge mass are very wasteful with their fuel and have shorter life spans than our own Sun. The Sun can continue shining for billions of years even though it burns 620 million tons of hydrogen into 617 million tons of helium every second.

How far away are the nearest stars?

The Sun is about 93 million miles from the Earth. The Sun's light, which travels at a speed of 186,000 miles per second, takes 8.32 minutes to reach the Earth. Sunlight takes more than 5 hours to reach the most distant planets in our solar system, Neptune and Pluto. The distance to the stars isn't measured in light minutes or even light hours, but in many, many light years. Our nearest neighbor star,

SPEED OF LIGHT

The speed of light or of radio waves in a vacuum is 186,282 miles per second — in actual conditions it is approximately 186,000 miles per second. This is the fastest that communications or radiant energy — radio and light waves — can travel. Spaceships can't reach this speed.

MEASURING DISTANCES IN SPACE is complicated. The distance from the Earth to the Moon or to Mars can be measured by bouncing a radar signal off their surfaces. The time it takes for the signal to return tells us how far away the object is. It is harder to determine the distance of stars. In June, a very distant star is always seen in a slightly different position than it is in December, when the Earth is at the opposite extreme of its orbit around the Sun. The closer a star is to Earth, the more its position varies during a six-month period. Using this change in position scientists can calculate the distance to the star.

The Hubble Space Telescope took these pictures of regions where new stars are being formed. Pictures taken in space are much clearer than anything taken on Earth.

Proxima Centauri, is 4.4 light years away. That's 25.86 trillion (25,860,000,000,000) miles away. Today's fastest space probes, which take a few days to reach the Moon and a few years to reach our neighboring planets, would need about 70,000 years to reach Proxima Centauri. Even if we could make them travel a hundred times faster, it would still take them 700 years to arrive! Many generations of space travelers would be born in these spaceships, and would live and die there before their descendants arrived in the year 2700. This example makes it clear that what we now proudly call "space exploration" will never be much more than a journey around our own cosmic backyard, the solar system. Given the current state of our technology we are still a very long way from the "Starship Enterprise."

Still, thanks to large telescopes and numerous space probes, we really know quite a lot about the stars and the universe, despite the gigantic distances involved.

In huge gas clouds like this, new stars and planetary systems are being formed even today. An Earth-bound observatory in the United States took this picture.

How are stars created?

Stars only have a limited amount of fuel, and therefore can't go on shining forever. Just like our own Sun, the stars didn't always exist but came into being at some time in the past and will go out when their fuel is used up.

New stars are being formed all the time. They are created out of gigantic clouds of gas and dust. A

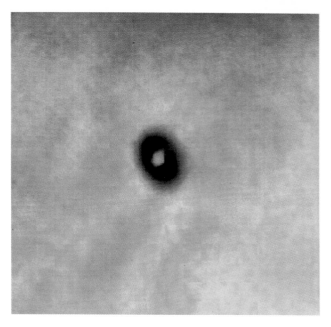

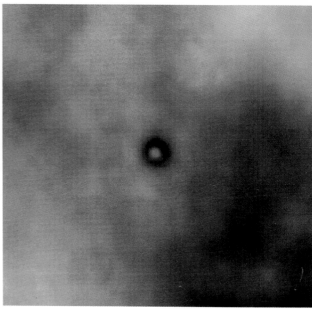

huge, cold cloud of cosmic gas, containing enough material to build thousands of new suns, begins to contract. After a time, this cloud breaks up into many smaller clouds. Within these smaller clouds areas of more concentrated matter begin to form, at first as balls of gas that are still fairly cold. These balls contract more and more, growing hotter and hotter in the process. Each of these areas of concentrated matter can develop into an individual star or even an entire star system.

Such balls of gas become smaller and denser, since they contract under the attraction of their own gravity. Other matter nearby rains down onto the growing star — a "protostar." At first the protostar is surrounded by a kind of atmosphere that light can't penetrate. As it gets hotter and hotter, however, it begins emitting visible light. Eventually the temperature in the center of the protostar heats up to several million degrees and the internal pressure reaches extreme levels. These are the conditions necessary for the beginning of

nuclear fusion, which releases almost unimaginable amounts of energy. The young star can now rely on its almost never-ending source of energy, its own nuclear fusion reactor. With this energy source many stars can continue to shine for billions of years.

Today we also have a good idea of the way planets are created. Most protostars rotate around an axis. As they contract, this rotation grows faster and faster. We see this same effect when ice skaters perform spins: they turn faster and faster as they pull their arms in close to their bodies. As this ball of hot gases rotates faster and faster, it flattens out into a disk. In the middle of the disk a huge amount of matter contracts into a dense ball and — as we saw above — becomes a radiant star. Planets form from the material in the disk.

Our own solar system probably came about like this. With today's large telescopes and modern satellites scientists can easily see large disks surrounding young stars. Planets and moons may also be formed from these disks in the future.

Thanks to the Hubble Space Telescope we can now observe the formation of new stars directly. This series of four pictures shows how disks of gas and dust form around young stars, disks that will later become planets and moons. The Earth was formed from just such a disk.

BROWN DWARVES

A young star must have at least 8% of the Sun's mass to become a real fixed star. If it is smaller than that, its center can't get hot enough to trigger nuclear fusion — the transformation of hydrogen into helium. A "would-be" sun like this is called a "brown dwarf" because it gives off a dark orange glow for a while, which appears brown from our distant vantage-point.

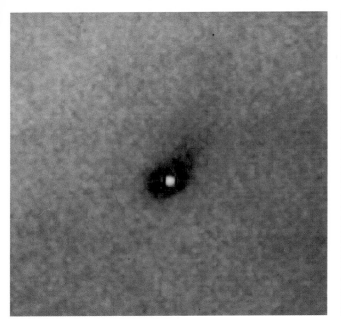

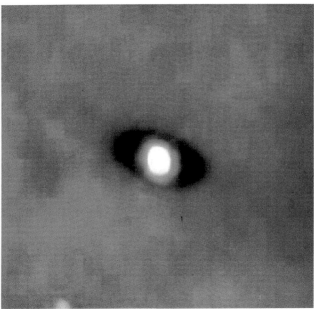

OUR SUN HAS FUEL for some 11 billion years, and about 5 billion have already passed. Before the Sun dies, it will become a "red giant," swallowing up Mercury and Venus and heating the Earth to more than 1,800° F.

At the end of their lives stars swell up to become red giants or super giants. They finally end up as white dwarves, neutron stars, or black holes.

What happens when a star dies?

When a star like our Sun is born, it can continue to shine at the same brightness for billions of years. At some point in the future, however, this star will have burned up all of the fuel at its core and will go dark. When all the hydrogen in its center has been turned into helium, it will begin to shrink, getting hotter and hotter. The hydrogen further away from the center now burns up as well and forms more helium. Finally, another nuclear fusion takes place and the helium is transformed into carbon. A tremendous pressure builds up inside the aging star and it expands into a "red giant." Finally the outer layer of the dying sun will drift off into space. A more massive star blows off its outer layer in a gigantic, violent explosion — it "goes supernova."

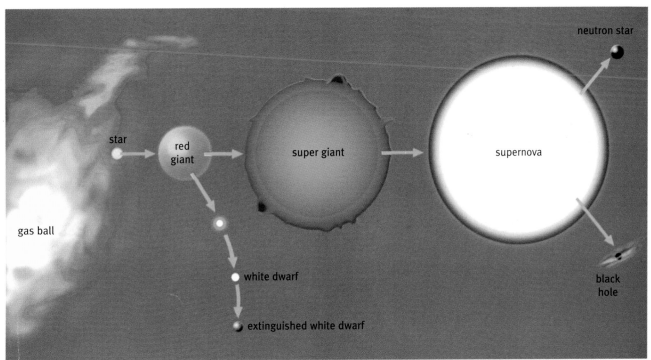

gas ball

star

red giant

super giant

supernova

neutron star

white dwarf

extinguished white dwarf

black hole

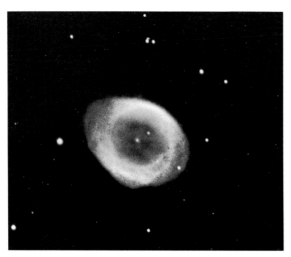

Here a dying sun has blown off its outer shell. The remaining core of the star will shrink into an unbelievably dense white dwarf.

are only about 12 miles in diameter. A teaspoonful of this material would weigh about 50 billion tons on Earth!

These remnants of stars are known as "neutron stars," since they are made almost entirely of subatomic particles called neutrons. Astronomers have identified many neutron stars. These tiny but extremely heavy spheres rotate at very high speed. There are regions on a neutron star that emit an unusually high amount of radiation. Whenever one of these regions rotates toward the Earth we receive a flash of radiation. To us it looks like a pulsing light source. This is why neutron stars are also called "pulsars."

1 SOLAR MASS is the basic unit astronomers use when measuring the mass of stars. This unit is equal to the mass of our Sun.

RADIATION is any type of wave emitted by a star — it can be particles, light, or heat.

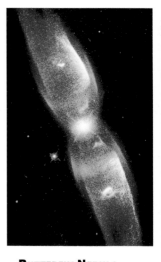

BUTTERFLY NEBULA
Gas shells given off by dying stars can take on all kinds of shapes, as can be seen from this picture taken by the Hubble Space Telescope.

What are white dwarves and pulsars?

Smaller stars like the Sun lose their outer layer gradually. Larger stars explode violently at the end of their lives, though usually a burnt-out core remains. If this core is less than 1.4 times the mass of the Sun (or 1.4 "solar masses"), it will become a white dwarf, a globe about the same size as the Earth. In this small ball, however, there is as much mass as in an entire sun. This means that just a teaspoon full of white dwarf material would weigh many tons!

The fate of burnt-out cores with a mass from 1.4 to 3 times the mass of the Sun is even more incredible. They contract until they

What is a black hole?

Although astronomers can still see the remains of stars that had less than 3 times the mass of our Sun, the remnants of stars that were more than 3 times the Sun's mass are invisible. They collapse into such a tiny volume that the gravity on their surfaces is unimaginable. It becomes so strong that it pulls everything toward its surface, even

The comparison below gives an idea of the relative sizes of bodies in space: red giants are much bigger than stars. White dwarves and neutron stars are incredibly tiny in comparison.

Star	White Dwarf	Neutron Star	Black Hole

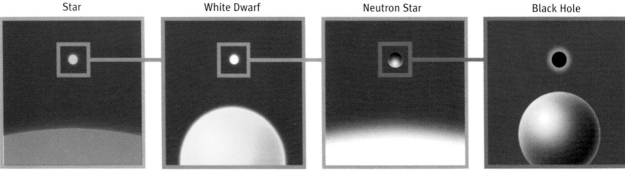

Red Giant	Star	White Dwarf	Neutron Star

A visible star orbiting a black hole. The black hole pulls in some of the star's matter and this matter becomes extremely hot in the process.

light. This makes it impossible for us to see this kind of collapsed star, which is why it is called a "black hole." Black holes work like a giant drain, sucking in everything that gets close enough and allowing nothing to escape – not even light.

Since black holes don't radiate any light, they can't be directly observed. Still, astronomers believe they have found proof of their existence. There are, for example, visible stars that seem to rotate around an invisible partner. This invisible partner can only be a black hole. The black hole draws matter from its partner star.

This matter heats up intensely as it flows toward the black hole and emits X-rays before it is swallowed up.

In addition to the "stellar" black holes, which are presumably the remains of stars, there are probably also black holes at the center of galaxies, black holes with an unimaginably dense mass. Many researchers — the British physicist Stephen Hawking, for example — believe that there are also "mini black holes." Theorists think these mini black holes probably stem from the very beginnings of the universe.

into particles — concentrations of greater and smaller amounts of matter form and evolve into groups of hundreds or even thousands of suns and planetary systems. Such star groups may become "open" star clusters, like the Seven Sisters. These are simply families of young stars that were born together out of the same large cloud of gases. In the beginning they follow a common path, but as they grow older they separate from the group. The globular clusters are some of the most beautiful objects in the universe. There aren't simply hundreds or even thousands of stars in a globular cluster, but hundreds of thousands or even millions of stars concentrated together. The stars at the center of a globular cluster are so tightly packed that they occasionally collide with each other. Most globular clusters are among the oldest objects in the universe.

This magnificent binary star cluster, located in the constellation Perseus, is visible to the naked eye — even though it is about 8,000 light years away. It contains about 1,000 stars.

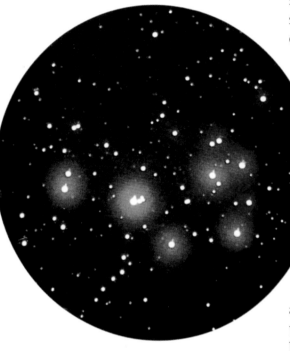

Pleiades, or the "Seven Sisters," is one of the best-known open star clusters. It is about 390 light years away and contains not 7 but rather about 200 stars.

Globular star clusters contain over 100,000 stars. They are so tightly packed at their center that the stars there often collide. They are among the oldest objects in the universe.

What are star clusters?

If you look carefully at the night sky, there are some places where the stars are more concentrated — you can see this even with the naked eye. These concentrations are called star clusters. The most famous one is the Seven Sisters or "Pleiades." It contains more than 7 stars, however — in fact, there are about 200.

In the regions where stars form – huge gas clouds that are decaying

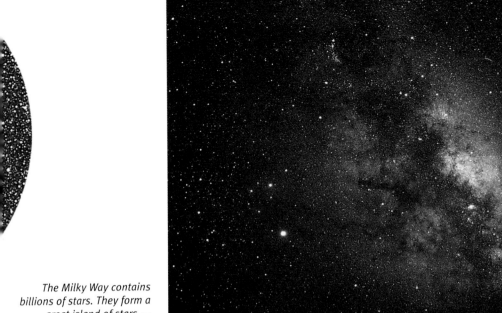

The Milky Way contains billions of stars. They form a great island of stars — our galaxy. We can only see a small part of our galaxy.

STAR-GAZING WITH BINOCULARS

A good pair of binoculars can easily reveal the miracles of the night sky. Looking into the Milky Way, we can see thousands of distant suns. We can even see many impressive star clusters and nebulae using normal binoculars. In order to find groups of stars like this, you will probably need a star map or guide. You can buy these at bookstores and observatories.

Where in the universe are we?

On a clear night, away from the lights of the city, you can see the silvery band of stars we call the Milky Way. In ancient times, people imagined these stars as the milk of a goddess, flowing across the heavens. If you look at the Milky Way through a pair of binoculars, you will see that it is made up of countless individual stars. All of these distant suns are part of a gigantic disk-shaped system, our galaxy, the Milky Way. Our own Sun is only an average star at the edge of this great island of stars. Dark areas in the Milky Way aren't empty space. In such places, huge clouds of dust absorb the light from the stars beyond.

We can imagine the Milky Way something like a rotating disk with a huge concentration at the center and many curved "arms" spiraling out from it. It is made up of about 200 billion stars, some gases and dust, and something astronomers call "dark matter," a kind of matter we know little about. Some 90% of our galaxy is made of this mysterious dark matter — the stars and planets make up only a minor part.

The stars in the Milky Way are concentrated in spiraling arms; these arms also contain many of the areas where new stars are formed — bright, young stars. If you were to look at these spiral arms from the outside, they would appear brighter than the rest of the disk. The disk is surrounded by a huge cloud consisting of globular clusters, individual stars, gas, and dark matter. This cloud is called the "halo."

The distance from one side of the disk to the other is about 100,000 light years. The thickness of the disk is about 18,000 light years at the center and 3,000 light years at the edges. The Sun is about 30,000 light years from the center of the galaxy, which it circles every 220 million years. At the center of the disk astronomers believe there is an unusual concentration of matter — a black hole.

In the outer parts of the disk, where our Sun and its planets are located, the concentration of stars is so thin that neighboring suns are light years apart. Collisions between stars can't really happen here. If we look in the direction of the galaxy's plane we see many stars and they look like a wide band of stars — the Milky Way. If we look out at a perpendicular to the galactic disk we see very few stars. We are looking out into the depths of space, where astronomers are constantly finding new surprises. We can only see a small part of our galaxy using telescopes. Dust clouds hide the rest. It is one of the greatest achievements of astronomy that scientists have been able to explore the structure of our galaxy. At the beginning of the 20th century astronomers still had no idea how big the galaxy was. Only with the help of radio astronomy were they able to discover what its shape was and that it was rotating.

The solar system and the galaxy

| What is dark matter? |

have one thing in common: at their centers they both have a large concentration of mass with stars or planets rotating around it in a plane. The further away a planet is from the Sun, the slower it orbits the Sun. The Earth circles the Sun at an average speed of 18.4 miles per second, while

distant Pluto has an average speed of 2.8 miles per second. Astronomers expected to find the same pattern in the galaxy. The further a star is from the center of the disk, the slower its orbit should be. This is not the case, however. The outermost stars in the galactic disk move much too quickly for this to be true. The only way scientists can explain this phenomenon is by assuming that there is much more matter in the Milky Way than we once thought. In addition to the visible stars and dust clouds, there must be huge amounts of dark matter. We can't see it — we know it exists only because of the gravity it exerts.

Many scientists believe dark matter consists almost entirely of unknown nuclear particles. It is also possible that dark matter is made up of small black holes.

The Milky Way is a giant disk containing gas, dust, dark matter, and about 200 billion stars. Our solar system is far away from the center of the disk.

THE CENTER OF THE MILKY WAY and the inner regions of our galaxy cannot be seen with an optical telescope since clouds of dust block our view. This dust doesn't block infrared or radio waves, however, and instruments that measure these rays allow us to learn about this hidden center. The movements of stars and gases has led scientists to conclude that there is a black hole of approximately 2 million solar masses at the center of the Milky Way.

THE MOST DISTANT OBJECTS we can see with the naked eye are galaxies. In the Southern hemisphere the Magellanic Clouds are visible. These are two companion galaxies of our Milky Way. They are around 200,000 light years away, and from Earth they look like they are part of the Milky Way. In the Northern hemisphere we can see the Andromeda galaxy, which is about 3 million light years away. To the naked eye it looks like a weak spot of light.

Scientists once thought neutrinos had no mass, but if they do, the quantity of neutrinos is unimaginably large, and their combined mass might make up this dark matter. Even "brown dwarves" might play a role. They are small stars that didn't get hot enough at the center to start nuclear fusion. As a result, they didn't become suns and grew cold. Since they don't shine, they are hard to locate.

Are there other galaxies?

Until the beginning of the 20th century, people thought that the Milky Way was unique. Now we know there are more than one hundred billion galaxies just in the part of the universe we can study! Each one contains billions or even trillions of stars and countless planets — some may support life.

Galaxies come in different shapes. The Milky Way is a "spiral galaxy" and so is the Andromeda Nebula. There are also galaxies with bar-shaped cores — they are called "barred spiral galaxies." Other galaxies are shaped like a ball — sometimes a flattened ball — and are called "elliptical galaxies." There are even a few that have a totally chaotic shape. These are called "irregular galaxies."

The centers of some galaxies emit huge amounts of radiation. Astronomers believe there are huge "galactic black holes" at the center of such galaxies. These black holes suck in tremendous amounts of matter. As the matter speeds up on its way into the black hole, it gets very hot. When it reaches very high temperatures it begins to emit strong radiation. Quasars are probably young, very active galaxies. The black hole in the center of a quasar is still surrounded by lots of matter, which it begins to swallow up. Since the black hole swallows so much matter it also sends out more radiation than other black holes. Quasars are some of the most distant objects in the universe. From Earth we see only the intensely bright center. It looks like a star, but is actually brighter than billions of stars together.

The Hubble Space Telescope has taken many pictures of distant galaxies. At first the pictures were fuzzy because of an error in the lens.

After astronauts repaired the space telescope, it began sending very sharp images of distant galaxies back to Earth.

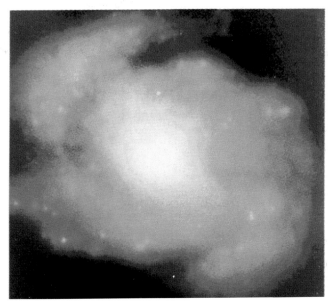

Planets and stars form families —

What do we know about the distribution of galaxies in space?

or systems, as astronomers call them. The Moon and Earth are a small "family" within our solar system. There are systems with two or more stars, called "binary" or "multiple systems." There are also clusters with 100 to 100,000 "family members." Galaxies are systems containing billions or trillions of suns. Galaxies are also grouped into systems.

The Milky Way, for example, has two satellite galaxies, the Magellanic Clouds. This small system belongs to a cluster of galaxies, called the "Local Group." Although the Local Group only contains about 30 galaxies, there are galactic clusters with thousands of individual galaxies. The Virgo cluster is one of these. It contains about 6,000 galaxies. But it doesn't stop there! Galaxies combine into even larger systems, known as "superclusters." Our Local Group belongs to the Virgo supercluster.

HOBBY ASTRONOMERS often have such good equipment nowadays that they can observe hundreds of galaxies and take photographs of them. Many hobby astronomers belong to astronomers' clubs. Some also travel to other countries where the view may be better.

TYPES OF GALAXIES

Elliptical Galaxy

Barred Spiral Galaxy

Spiral Galaxy

Elliptical Galaxy

Barred Spiral Galaxy

Spiral Galaxy

Spiral Galaxy

Irregular Galaxy

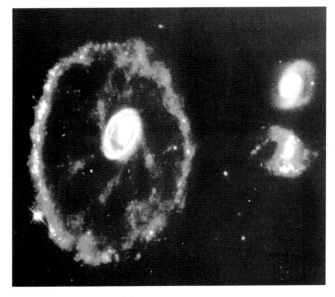

Galaxies sometimes collide. The Hubble Space Telescope photographed one of these collisions. A small, compact galaxy sped through a larger spiral galaxy and transformed it into an enormous "wagon wheel" in which millions of new stars are now forming.

To their surprise, scientists have discovered that these systems are not evenly spread throughout the universe. Instead, they seem to lie in large planes or curves, almost like walls. Between these walls there are enormous spaces that are almost entirely empty. The discovery of these structures in the universe is one of the most important discoveries of the 20th century.

At the center of large galaxy clusters the groupings of stars are especially dense. Here it is not uncommon for galaxies to collide with one another. The larger galaxy then swallows many of the stars that used to belong to the smaller galaxy. Astronomers then speak of "galactic cannibalism."

View of a galaxy cluster. Many of these clusters contain thousands of large and small galaxies.

How fast do galaxies move?

If we ignore the closer neighbor galaxies, like the Andromeda Nebula, all distant galaxies have one thing in common: they are moving away from us. The further they are away from us, the faster they are moving. The universe is expanding. But it's not as if we were at the center of an explosion, where the individual fragments fly away from the center. The entire space in which the galaxies are embedded is expanding. The galaxies are a little like raisins in bread dough that is "rising." The distance between the raisins increases even though the raisins themselves are not actively moving — the dough is expanding and carrying them with it. Nevertheless, if we were in any one of the many galaxies it would seem to us as if we were in the middle of a great explosion and all the fragments were flying away from us!

Galactic super clusters are not evenly spread throughout space. Astronomers were surprised to discover that they occur on the walls of large "bubbles."

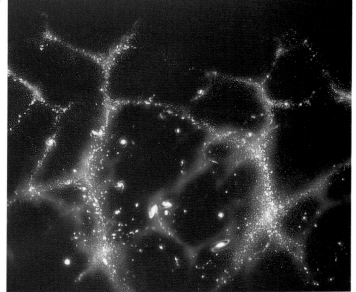

The scientist who first proved there are other galaxies and that these galaxies are moving away from us was astronomer Edwin Hubble (1889 – 1953). The Hubble Space Telescope was named after him. The universe is expanding according to "Hubble's Law": twice the distance means twice the speed. The speed of galaxies increases the further away they are.

How can we measure the speed of galaxies? Astronomers use the "Doppler effect." The sound of an airplane's engines seems higher pitched when it is flying towards us than when it is flying away from us. This is true in general. If a wave source is moving toward us its waves are higher pitched — they have a shorter wave length — than when the source isn't moving at all. If the source is moving away from us its waves are lower pitched — they have a longer wavelength. This is the Doppler effect. It also

applies to light, which can likewise be described as waves. The faster a star is moving towards us, the shorter the wavelength of its light. The faster a star is moving away from us, the longer the wavelength of its light. From this difference in wavelength, scientists can calculate the speed of the wave source. In this way they found that some stars are moving away from us and others towards us. This is not true of galaxies, however. Nearly all distant galactic systems show an increase in wavelength — they are all moving away from us.

If they are all moving away from each other, then they must have been closer together at some point in the past. Long ago, the universe must have been a concentrated ball of fire that then began to expand and to cool down. Most scientists believe the universe had a beginning, and they call it the "big bang."

Edwin Hubble was one of the 20th century's greatest astronomers and explorers. The Hubble Space Telescope was named after him.

EDWIN HUBBLE started working at the Mount Wilson Observatory in California in 1919. He was the first person to prove that there are other galaxies outside of our own Milky Way. His most important discovery was that the universe is constantly expanding. This again led to the conclusion that there must have been a big bang. Hubble also investigated the gas clouds in our Milky Way.

The universe is expanding. The greater the distance between two galaxies, the faster they move apart. Edwin Hubble discovered this phenomenon.

A Beginning — and No Ending?

Comets are gigantic "dirty snowballs" that begin to evaporate and give off dust particles when they pass near a star. This material forms the comet's tail, which can quickly change in brightness and shape.

ESTIMATING THE AGE OF ROCKS

Many nuclei disintegrate at a certain speed. A certain type of uranium — uranium 238 — disintegrates into lead. Starting with one ounce of uranium 238, only 1/2 ounce is left after 4.47 billion years. If a rock contains uranium 238, its age can be deduced from the uranium-lead ratio. If half of the original uranium has disintegrated then the stone must be 4.47 billion years old.

How old is our solar system?

If you study the night sky regularly for several years, you might think that the stars and planets have existed forever and that they never change. Long ago the ancient Greeks and Romans saw the planet Venus as an evening or morning star, and enjoyed the soft light of the full Moon. Humans identified the constellation Scorpius thousands of years ago and there is no record of any change. And yet, even in the short span of a human lifetime it is possible to see changes in space. Occasionally a comet sweeps across the sky, drawing its majestic tail along, and then disappears again. Now and then one of the dimmer stars becomes a billion times brighter than

before: we are witnessing an enormous galactic explosion, the birth of a "supernova."

There are also very different kinds of observations that show us that there is change in the universe, that stars and planets are created and can also perish. The Earth's rocks were formed at different times — some are very young, some very old. Today there are methods for determining the age of rock samples, methods that would work even if the rocks were more than 10 billion years old. We have never found any rocks on our planet that were more than 4 billion years old, however. The same is true for Moon rocks and meteorites. Meteorites are lumps of rock that originate all over our solar system and occasionally fall to Earth. Some meteorites were bro-

Meteorites are rocks or lumps of iron that come from other parts of our solar system and fall to Earth. They break off from larger objects such as planets or asteroids when these collide with other objects.

Astronauts brought back Moon rocks from the Apollo expeditions. Scientists were then able to determine the age of these rocks in laboratories on Earth.

ken off from Mars by collisions; others are fragments of asteroids or planetoids. Meteorites often look very different, but they all have one thing in common: none are more than about 4.5 billion years old. It doesn't matter where in our solar system they come from, there seems to be a maximum age limit. This evidence suggests that our immediate neighborhood in the universe — our solar system — can't be any older than about 4.5 billion years.

There is another reason for thinking that our solar system has a limited age: the Sun only has enough fuel for about 11 billion years. After that, it will have used up all the hydrogen in its center. In

other words, the solar system can't possibly be more than 11 billion years old. There are many indications that the Sun has been shining for about 5 billion years, and that it still has about 6 billion years to go.

Has our galaxy always existed?

In the last few decades astronomers have developed methods for finding out the age of star clusters. We know that stars with tremendous mass live for a relatively short time, and that smaller, dimmer stars live for a very long time. If a star cluster has many of these huge, short-lived stars it can't be very old, since all the stars in the cluster were

The center of a star cluster, photographed by the Hubble Space Telescope. Star systems like this help astronomers to estimate the age of our galaxy. (Far left: a view of the entire star cluster)

ATOMS are often compared to solar systems. The nucleus is the "Sun" and the electrons are the "planets" circling it. The nucleus is tiny and often has to be shown much larger than life to be visible at all (as in our picture below). If you imagine the nucleus to be as big as a dime, then the entire atom, with its electron cloud, would be as big as the Empire State Building! Unlike planets, electrons can only move along set paths.

An atom consists of a tiny nucleus orbited by electrons. The nucleus contains protons and neutrons — both of which are made up of quarks.

formed at more or less the same time. On the other hand, if all the large and medium sized stars have disappeared from a cluster, then it must be very old.

The Milky Way is surrounded by globular clusters. Using the method described above, astronomers have succeeded in determining the approximate ages of these clusters. Their results were very surprising! These globular clusters must have formed over 12 billion years ago. This means they are the oldest objects in the Milky Way system, which is thus more than 10 billion years old but still not infinitely old.

The Milky Way had a beginning and has existed much longer than our solar system. We will see below that this has to be the case, since the Sun and the Earth contain elements that didn't exist in the beginning. These elements formed over the course of the first few bil-

lion years after the creation of the universe.

We have already seen that galaxies are moving apart and that the universe is constantly expanding. We know approximately how far away from us many of these galaxies are. We can also measure the speed at which these galaxies are moving away from us. Using this information we can at least estimate when this expansion began — when the universe, in its present form, came into being. The age we come up with is about 15 billion years. This figure is only approximate, of course. We don't know, for example, if the speed of the universe's expansion has changed over time. It's also difficult to measure exactly how far away galaxies are. The different "standard candles" (a measure of light intensity) people use lead to different results. This is always a source of confusion and causes a great deal of debate. Almost all scientists agree, however, that the universe in its present form must have come into being many billions of years ago.

If the galaxies are now moving away from each other, they must have been closer together in the past. Even further back in the past the matter in the universe must have been extremely compact. According to the laws of physics it must also have been very hot. Since planets, stars, galaxies and even atoms can't exist at extremely high temperatures, the young universe must have

How did the universe begin?

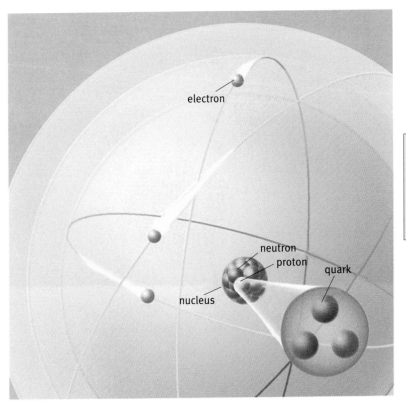

electron

neutron
proton
quark

nucleus

According to the "big bang" theory, the newly formed universe expanded extremely rapidly — a process known as "inflation." In the illustration above, an artist has attempted to show what this might have looked like.

nitely dense and hot point. Scientists call such a point a "singularity." This singularity must have started to expand explosively and to cool down. Scientists call this very first event the "big bang." In physics, there are no such singularities, and so we still don't really know what happened in the first fractions of a second of the universe's birth.

Most scientists do agree, however, that after the big bang ever more complicated forms emerged as time went on, forms like atoms, planets, suns, and finally — at least on Earth — life.

The course of our universe was set in the first fractions of a second after the big bang. The spans of time involved are so brief that our language can hardly describe them. In order to understand what happened in the

been nothing more than a mixture of hot, densely packed elementary particles and high energy radiation.

Elementary particles are smaller even than atoms. Atoms are composed of three kinds of particles: protons and neutrons form the nucleus, and electrons form the shell. Protons have a positive electrical charge, electrons have a negative one. Neutrons do not have an electrical charge — they are "neutral." Protons and neutrons are composed of even smaller particles called "quarks." As far as we know today, quarks and electrons cannot be divided or broken into smaller parts, which is why we call them elementary particles.

If we trace the history of the universe back even further, we eventually come to an absurd result: at time zero the universe must have been an infi-

POWERS OF TEN

In astronomy, we often have to deal with numbers that are so incredibly large or so immeasurably tiny that they are difficult to put into words. Instead of using trillions or writing numbers with, say, 12 zeros, astronomers often use powers of ten. The system is very easy: a 1 with 3 zeros (1,000) is called "10 to the power of 3," and written 10^3. A 1 with 9 zeros is 10^9, and a 1 with 18 zeros is 10^{18}. For example: the distance from the Earth to the Sun is 93 million miles or 93,000,000 miles. That's 93 x 10^6 miles. The small number written after the 10 is called the "exponent."

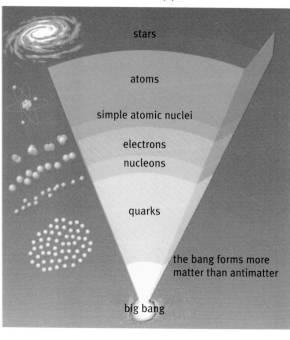

This diagram shows the history of the universe, beginning with the big bang. Gradually the elementary particles, nuclear building blocks, and simple atomic nuclei formed; then later complete atoms and stars.

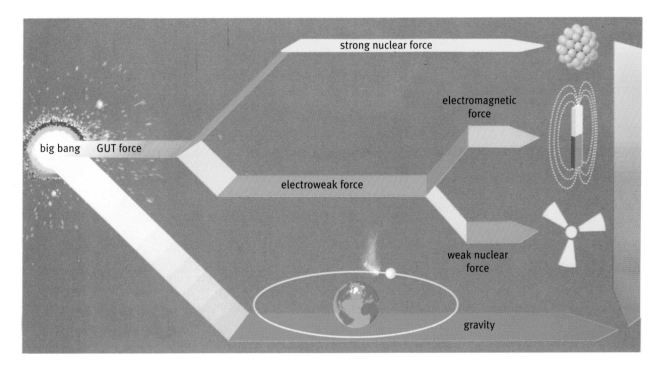

The four known fundamental forces — gravity, electromagnetism, strong nuclear force, and weak nuclear force might have developed from a single, original force.

VERY SMALL NUMBERS can be written with the same system, but using negative exponents. 1/1,000 is written as 10^{-3}, and we read it as "ten to the power of minus three." A millionth (1/1,000,000) is written 10^{-6}. An atomic nucleus is about 1/1,000,000,000,000 of an inch in diameter — 10^{-12}. A millionth of a second could also be written as 10^{-6} seconds.

first fractions of a second after the big bang we must first know that everything in the universe is held together by four forces. The gravity that causes an apple to fall to the ground and holds the Moon in its orbit around the Earth is one. Another is the electromagnetic force we see when magnetic poles attract or repel each other. We are all familiar with these forces. The other two forces are the weak and strong nuclear forces. These forces are only effective over short distances, but are very important. The strong nuclear force is particularly essential. It holds together the quarks in protons and neutrons, and keeps these protons and neutrons in the nucleus of the atom. We sometimes talk about a "nuclear force" that keeps the nucleus of the atom stable. Whereas the strong nuclear force and the electromagnetic force only affect certain particles, gravity and the weak nuclear force affect all elementary particles.

After the big bang, the newly born universe changed very rapidly. Scientists are working hard to determine what happened during the first 10^{-43} seconds — that's 0.0000000000000000000000000 00000000000000001 seconds! The infant universe was very simple at first. There was only one primal force and only one kind of particle for it to act on. 10^{-43} seconds after its birth, the universe was unimaginably hot — 10^{32} °F — and no more than 10^{-33} inches wide — far smaller than an elementary particle. The pressure and density were unimaginably high. Under such conditions physicists say there could only have been one kind of force and one kind of particle.

The universe then began to expand, and as it expanded it also cooled. 10^{-43} seconds after the birth of the universe, the single force

What happened at the very beginning of the universe?

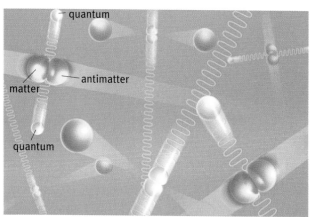

When antimatter and matter meet they destroy each other and are transformed into energy. This energy takes the form of radiation particles — so-called quanta.

split into two forces, gravity and the so-called "GUT" force. After about 10^{-35} seconds, the strong nuclear force separated from the GUT force, leaving only the electroweak force. After 10^{-12} seconds this force then split into the electromagnetic force and the weak nuclear force.

The elementary particles were formed at the same time as the fundamental forces. What was initially a very simple structure quickly became increasingly complicated. From about 10^{-35} to 10^{-32} seconds after the big bang the universe expanded very rapidly. This process is called "inflation." In this unbelievably brief stretch of time, the universe became 10^{90} times bigger than before.

After about a thousandth of a second nearly all the matter in the universe disappeared — it was converted into radiation. There were quarks and electrons, and also antiquarks and antielectrons. For every particle there is a corresponding antiparticle. The antiparticles are made of antimatter. If an elementary particle meets an antiparticle they destroy each other in a burst of radiation. Almost all of the quarks and antiquarks destroyed each other less than one thousandth of a second after the big bang. There was always slightly more matter than antimatter, however, so not all of the quarks were destroyed. The remaining quarks joined in groups of three to form either a proton or a neutron — the building blocks for the nuclei of atoms. In the next few minutes, most of the electrons and antielectrons also destroyed each other. At first the remaining electrons moved about freely in space. Later they formed shells around the atomic nuclei.

Once the components of the atoms had formed — in the first minutes after the birth of the universe — all the necessary building blocks for stars, planets, and life forms were present.

How were atoms formed?

Three minutes after the big bang, our universe was a mixture of radiation, protons, neutrons, and electrons, together with other particles — for example neutrinos. It had a temperature of about 1 billion degrees. The processes that followed during

PLASMA

Plasma is a mixture of "free" nuclei and electrons — ones not yet "captured" as part of an atom. This was the way these particles existed for the first 300,000 years of the life of our universe. Plasma is completely opaque. Atoms, however, are more or less transparent, even though they absorb some kinds of light. The young universe became transparent only after atoms had formed — until then it was completely opaque.

GUT stands for Grand Unified Theory. This theory describes how the different fundamental forces are related to each other.

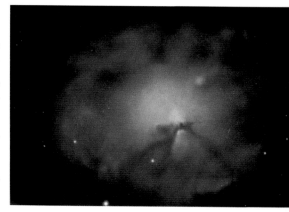

Many scientists think that our galaxy was formed from a ball-shaped cloud of gas (near right). Star clusters began to form in this cloud (center), and the rest became the disk of the Milky Way (far right).

The nucleus of a normal hydrogen atom: one proton

The nucleus of a deuterium atom: one proton + one neutron

The nucleus of a helium atom: 2 protons + 2 neutrons

There weren't any atoms immediately after the big bang, but only a hot mixture of protons, neutrons, and electrons. Protons and neutrons joined to form simple nuclei. Later the nuclei captured electrons and formed complete atoms. Hydrogen is the simplest atom – it contains only one proton and one electron.

During the next 100,000 years the universe continued to grow cooler and cooler. After 300,000 years its temperature was only around 5,400° F. At this temperature complete atoms could now begin to form. The atomic nuclei captured electrons, which from this point on orbited the nuclei. At higher temperatures this wouldn't have been possible. Temperature is, after all, just another way of saying how much energy the particles have and how fast they fly away from each other. At very high temperatures, the atoms would collide with each other, ejecting their electrons. Without electrons it is impossible to create complete atoms.

the next 30 minutes are already familiar to us from the fusion that takes place inside a star. "Nucleons" – protons and neutrons, that is – fused together to form atomic nuclei. The simplest kinds of nuclei were formed: hydrogen and helium nuclei. Trace amounts of lithium were also formed. Heavy nuclei like iron and oxygen could not form at first. They were formed much later, in the centers of stars.

How were the galaxies created?

There is much evidence that concentrations of matter started forming already when the universe was still very young. These concentrations were shaped a lot like the empty spaces now "walled" in by galaxies. These were probably the places where galaxies formed. The strong forces of attraction coming from these mysterious concentrations probably led to the formation of galaxies.

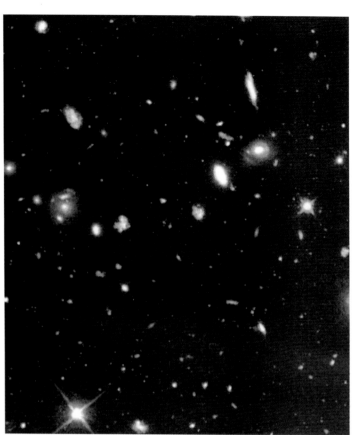

A glimpse into the distant past: The Hubble Space Telescope can discern very distant galaxies. We see them as they were billions of years ago when the universe was still young.

Many scientists believe our own galaxy, with its billions of stars, was once just a huge rotating ball of hydrogen, helium, and dark matter. The first star systems — the globular star clusters — formed within this ball. The rest of the huge ball of gas became smaller and smaller and turned faster and faster. Finally, the ball shape became flatter and flatter until the disk of today's Milky Way was eventually formed. We already know this process, on a smaller scale, from the way that stars form. A large concentration containing many stars began to form in the center. It is even possible that a huge black hole was created in the center of the galaxy. This black hole began to suck in sur-

rounding matter, and gathered more mass. More and more concentrations of matter began to form in the disk, and these later became star groups. New stars are being formed even today, although it happens much less often than when our universe was still young.

Today we can read the history of the formation of the Milky Way from its structure. A rotating disk extends out from its dense center, and this disk is surrounded by globular clusters, stars arranged in a globe shape. In the billions of years that followed, new stars were constantly being born. Many of them have enough fuel to burn for 50 billion years. Not the ones with the greatest mass, however. In their relatively brief existence they produced heavier and heavier nuclei — like those of iron and also of carbon, one of the

CHEMICAL ELEMENTS

Almost all matter consists of chemical elements such as iron, oxygen, and hydrogen. Atoms are the smallest units of the elements. The smallest unit of iron is an iron atom, the smallest unit of hydrogen is a hydrogen atom, etc. The number of protons in the nucleus determines the kind of element. Hydrogen atoms have 1 proton, carbon atoms have 6 and uranium atoms have 92 protons in their nuclei. Any nucleus with 6 protons is a carbon nucleus, no matter how many neutrons it has. Molecules consist of two or more atoms clinging together. Compounds contain atoms of two or more elements.

This picture shows an old star with a tremendous mass, exploding at the end of its life span. The outer layers of the supernova race away from the center. The remaining core may become a neutron star or a black hole.

Nuclei of heavy atoms (C: carbon, O: oxygen, Fe: iron) are released during the eruption of a supernova. These heavy nuclei didn't exist at the beginning of the universe — they were formed in the core of the star.

Here, too, a supernova has broken apart. Even after thousands of years, we can still see the remains of the exploded star mixed in with the surrounding gas.

these heavy atomic nuclei managed to capture electrons, thereby forming complete atoms.

When our solar system came into being about 4.6 billion years ago, heavier elements like oxygen and carbon already existed. Without these elements a planet like Earth can't exist. Every carbon atom in our bodies comes from a star that shone a long, long time ago before finally exploding or slowly blowing away its outer shell. In the process, elements like carbon were created. We can now see that our Sun must be much younger than the universe as a whole. Like the planets, the Sun contains elements that didn't exist in the beginning and were only available billions of years later.

Scientists are still debating the details of the formation of galaxies, and there may be great surprises to come. In the last few years, thanks to the Hubble Space Telescope, we have been able to observe very distant galaxies. These observations show that, over time, spiral galaxies have changed much more quickly than elliptical galaxies. Many of these star systems have been deformed or destroyed in collisions with other galaxies.

building blocks of life. As these stars exploded into supernovas, they hurled the heavy nuclei into space. Among these were very heavy nuclei like those of uranium. They can only be created by a supernova explosion. And so the gases in our galaxy slowly became enriched with carbon, nitrogen, and iron — elements that didn't even exist in the beginning. Some of

How was our solar system created?

The Milky Way was already about 7 billion years old when our solar system began to form about 4.6 billion years ago. The area where our own Sun was created was filled with thousands of other newly forming suns. Our solar system — the Sun, planets, and moons — was once nothing more than a large, slowly rotating ball of gas and dust. In addition to the elements that had "always" been there — like hydrogen and helium — this gas ball also contained a small percentage of heavy elements like iron and carbon.

This primal cloud began to contract, since the elements it was made of attracted each other. The cloud rotated faster and faster the smaller it got. It flattened out into a disk, and the center of the disk gave birth to the Sun. The planets were formed from outer parts of

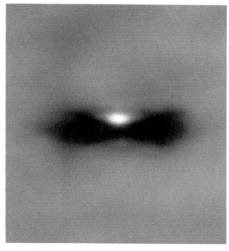

Here, before our very eyes, a planetary system is probably forming from this huge disk! The Hubble Space Telescope was able to photograph this event.

the disk. Larger and larger concentrations of matter began to clump together. The larger the concentration, the better it could attract matter from its neighbors. This is how the planets were formed.

Even if we still don't know all the details, the shape of our solar system shows us that it was formed from a disk. All of the large planets are located more or less on the same plane — the plane of the original disk. All of the planets rotate in the same direction, the same direction as the original cloud of gas and dust.

THE EARTH'S IRON CORE, its high levels of silicon, and its oxygen-rich atmosphere are a very unusual combination in the universe. It was made possible by events in our solar system's infancy. As the solar system developed, the Sun's intense rays blew much of the hydrogen outward. This left high concentrations of heavy elements nearer the center — where the Earth is. Further out large hydrogen balls gathered around small, dense concentrations of matter, forming planets like Jupiter and Saturn.

The Earth about 4 billion years ago. The primal atmosphere and the first oceans had formed. Meteorites rained down constantly. In the atmosphere organic matter began to form.

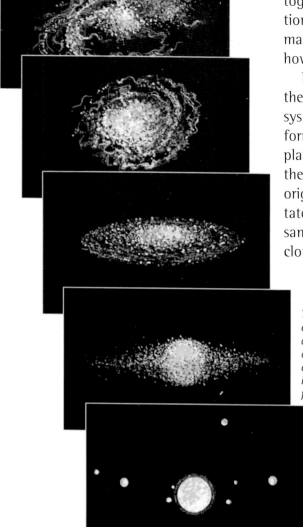

The emergence of a solar system: a cloud of gas and dust begins to contract. It flattens into a disk. The sun forms in the center and the planets form in the disk.

Some theorists claim that life was brought to Earth from some other part of the universe. The basic materials from which life on Earth then developed were supposed to be tiny, single celled life forms brought to our planet in fragments of comets or meteorites. We can't rule this out as a possibility. This would only transfer the mystery of the origin of life to another planet, however.

Why is there life on Earth?

At first the Earth was probably nothing more than a ball of molten rock and metal. The high temperature came from the huge amounts of highly radioactive metals it still contained. These metals released tremendous energy. The Earth was still contracting, and this also created energy, as did the impact of meteorites. Heavier elements like nickel and iron sank into the molten Earth and formed its core. The mantel formed around the core and the crust formed on the outside. The crust eventually cooled and became hard. Hot gases escaped from thousands of volcanoes and cracks in the Earth's crust and formed the first, primitive atmosphere, which contained substances like methane and water vapor. After more cooling, water rained down onto the young planet in violent cloudbursts, and formed the first oceans.

In this primal atmosphere, the rays of the Sun interacted with the elements to form large molecules — some of the building blocks of life. The first single-celled life forms probably developed from these molecules about 3.6 billion years ago. They were protected from the Sun's intense radiation by the primal oceans they lived in. And so life began on Earth.

Later, multicellular life-forms also developed, and about 500 million years ago they began to move onto land. In the meantime, a new layer had formed in the atmosphere — the ozone layer — and it protected life-forms on land

from the dangerous solar radiation. An amazing variety of creatures evolved in these 500 million years. Again and again, however, enormous collisions — with planetoids, for example — led to the extermination of up to 80 percent of these life-forms. The most famous of these catastrophes led to the extinction of the dinosaurs about 65 million years ago.

The history of humankind is very short compared to the history of the Earth. If we imagine the entire history of the Earth as one year, then the last 2,000 years of human history are equal to 14 seconds! This is why the Big Dipper looked exactly the same to the ancients Romans as it does to us today. Measured against the history of the universe, the entire existence of humanity has lasted no longer than the time needed for a "snapshot" — and snapshots don't record motion or change. If we could live for 100,000 years we would see changes in the constellations. Well-known stars would explode in this period of time and disappear from their constellations.

There are many bits of evidence

| Is there evidence for the big bang? |

supporting the "big bang" theory. One of these is the fact that the universe is expanding. The rate of expansion suggests that the universe began about 15 billion years ago. The levels of helium in the universe are also exactly what the theory would predict.

Another very important piece of evidence is the existence of background radiation. This is the light emitted by the very early universe when it first became transparent. The universe was very hot then, about 5,400° F, and radiated intense light. This light had a short wavelength at first, but stretched out as the universe expanded. It became microwave radiation, with a long wavelength. This radiation streams toward us from every direction, and was detected only a few decades ago. It is a signal from the time just after the big bang!

Of course this evidence doesn't convince all scientists and some reject the theory of the big bang as a one-time act of creation. One alternative theory says that the universe will only expand to a certain point before collapsing and shrinking again. It won't contract into an infinitely small space, however. When it reaches an extremely high concentration and temperature, it will "rebound" and begin to expand again. The evidence presented above for the big bang theory doesn't really contradict this idea. The rebound, also known as the "big bounce," is a lot like a big bang — but there have been many "bounces" and not just one.

For the sake of completeness we should also mention the "steady state" theory. According to it, there wasn't any beginning at all. The universe has always looked more or less the same according to this theory. As the universe expanded, new matter is supposed to have formed, so that the concentration of matter in the universe remained constant (steady state). Today only a very small number of scientists defend this theory. The evidence for some kind of beginning is too great.

THE MILLER EXPERIMENT
In 1953, a chemistry student named Stanley Miller conducted an experiment that is now famous. He managed to reconstruct conditions as they had been on Earth when it was still very young. He filled a glass container with water and added the same mixture of gases that had existed in the Earth's early atmosphere. Then he ran an electrical current through this controlled "environment" — imitating a bolt of lightning. Soon afterwards, organic molecules formed in the mixture — the basic elements of life!

THE BEGINNING OF LIFE
The Miller experiment does not explain the beginning of life itself, but only how some of the essential building blocks formed. He was able to show how amino acids — the basic elements of proteins — might have formed. Such large molecules could probably only form in the presence of iron pyrite. First an organic layer formed on the surface of the pyrite. Together with the pyrite, this layer was able to form complex molecules.

LIFE FROM THE OCEAN?
The most widely accepted theory says that life developed in the oceans. There isn't much evidence to support the theory that the inhabitants of distant planets brought the beginnings of life to Earth.

MAX PLANCK AND ALBERT EINSTEIN were two of the world's most important physicists. Einstein developed the "Theory of Relativity," which describes the relationship between energy and mass — like the energy in black holes. Planck's quantum theory describes the behavior of atoms and particles.

"PLANCK TIME" refers to the first 10^{-43} seconds after the big bang. So far, no one has succeeded in developing a workable theory that can explain what happened in the universe during this first tiny fraction of a second. Such a theory would have to combine Planck's quantum theory and Einstein's theory of relativity, and this has not been possible so far.

Have space and time always existed?

If you read some descriptions of the big bang you might get the idea that it was some kind of explosion where fragments were blown out into space that already existed. People often ask what existed before the big bang. When they ask this, they are assuming that time and space have always existed. Physicists, however, believe that space and time only came into existence with the big bang. Before the big bang, space and time weren't clearly defined or distinguishable. We have to realize that everything — space and time as well — came into being with the big bang. In the course of the newly created time, the newly created space began to expand.

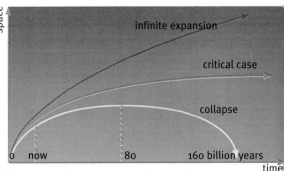

The universe is expanding, and, depending on the density of matter it contains, it may collapse into itself (closed universe), it may come to a halt after an infinite amount of time (the "critical case"), or it may continue to expand forever (open universe).

Infinite expansion — or collapse?

The expansion of the universe is slowing down more and more with time. This is because the gravitational forces of galaxies and dark matter attract and slow each other. This raises the question whether the universe will one day stop expanding and collapse into itself. Whether or not this is possible, depends on the concentration of matter in the uni-

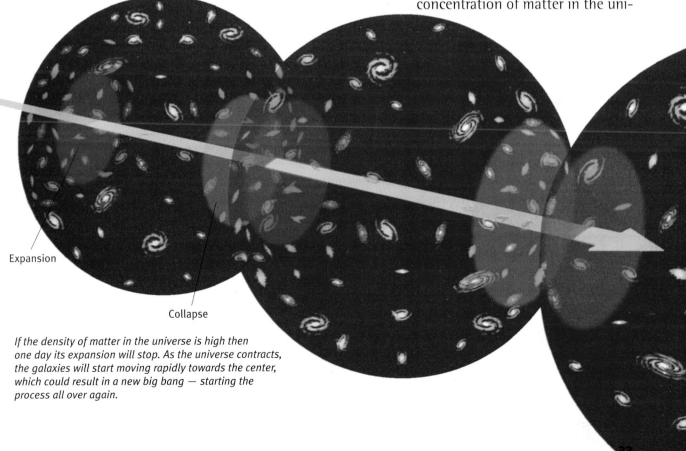

Expansion

Collapse

If the density of matter in the universe is high then one day its expansion will stop. As the universe contracts, the galaxies will start moving rapidly towards the center, which could result in a new big bang — starting the process all over again.

verse. If it is very high, then the attractive forces should be strong enough to stop the expansion. If the concentration is low then the mass will slow down, but it won't come to a stop or begin contracting. The density of the matter in the universe would have to exceed a specific "critical value" — also called "closure density" — if the expanding universe is going to collapse.

If we take only the visible galaxies with their stars and gas clouds, then there isn't nearly enough matter to bring the universe to a stop and cause it to collapse. In addition to the visible bodies in space, however, there must be a great deal of dark matter. This dark matter probably makes up between 90 and 99 percent of the universe. Astronomers have only begun to study dark matter, but one thing is certain: it exerts a force of attraction! It is also possible that this is enough to stop the expansion of the universe. In something like 90 to 180 billion years then, the universe would reach a state much like it was at the time of the big bang. All matter would again be concentrated into a dense, hot ball of fire from which a new universe could arise. This massive collapse with its "final bang" is called the "big crunch."

From what we know today, however, there is not quite enough matter in the universe, even with dark matter, to reach closure density. There is much evidence that we are balanced at the density boundary and that the universe will continue to expand. Only after an almost infinite time, first predicted by Einstein, will it come to a stop.

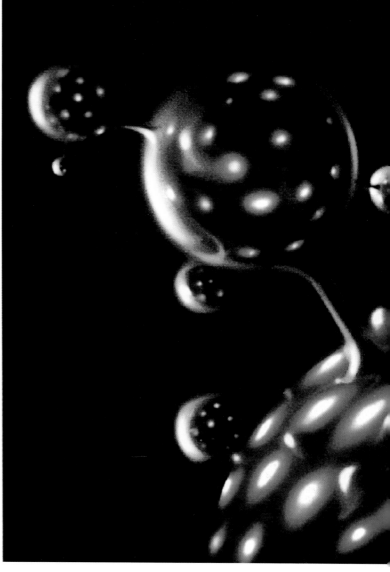

What will the universe look like in the future?

According to our present-day knowledge, which is nowhere near complete, the universe will continue expanding. In about 6 billion (or 6.0×10^9) years our Sun will die out, having used all of its fuel. Only the distant planets in our solar system will survive the Sun's collapse and continue orbiting the remaining white dwarf. There are always new stars being formed, however, and many of them will live much longer than our Sun. At some point, however, there will be no more matter from which to form new stars. At an even later point —

Is our universe the only one of its kind? Are there "parallel universes" that we could reach through so-called "wormholes"? It is possible, but we still have no proof of their existence.

TIME PASSES MORE SLOWLY on a very fast spaceship than it does on Earth, according to Einstein. If a spaceship orbited at 99.94% of the speed of light, 68 years would pass on the spaceship while 2,000 years passed on Earth. For a light particle moving at exactly the speed of light, time stands still. Time only exists for matter moving slower than light. Before there was matter, there was no time.

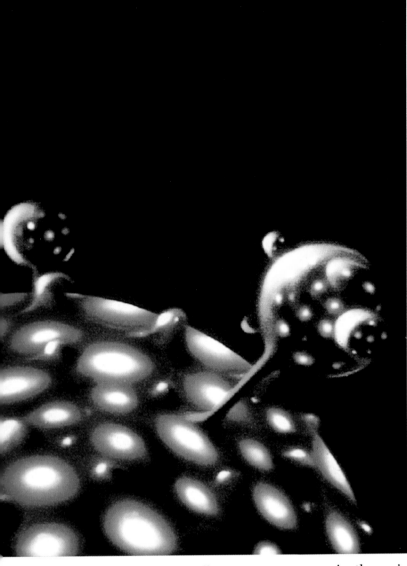

There are even theories that predict that one day all the matter in the universe will have decayed. The protons will have been destroyed after about 10^{33} years, the black holes formed from stars in about 10^{65} years, and the galactic black holes in 10^{100} years. Only electrons, neutrinos, and radiation particles will remain. The universe would have become nearly empty — only every 500,000 light years or so could you find an elementary particle. The universe would be approaching a state of "eternity," in which even time itself would no longer exist.

How does God fit into the big bang theory?

For many religions the beginning of the world looks something like this: out of a simple, primal state, the stars, the Earth, animals, plants, and finally humans came into being. Physicists also see the development of the universe in a similar way. Out of a primal ball of fire came elementary particles, atoms, galaxies, suns, planets, complex molecules, and finally life. Even if the big bang really happened as described above, this still doesn't tell us whether it was the act of a creator — and would then be proof of God's existence — or if it was simply a fluctuation in the primal vacuum of space. Physics can neither prove nor disprove the existence of God. When scientists study atoms and galaxies it still doesn't tell us whether they were created by a higher being or not. It is entirely possible to study quarks and black holes and still believe in God.

A UNIVERSE MADE TO MEASURE?

Some scientists believe that the universe was arranged from the very start so that human life could evolve. If the expansion after the big bang had been even 1/100,000 slower than it actually was, the universe would probably have collapsed again and no galaxies or suns could have formed. If the nuclear forces holding protons and neutrons together had been even slightly different, there wouldn't have been enough carbon formed to make life possible.

10^{12} years — every sun in the universe will have burned out. The universe will then be entirely dark and planets will orbit dead stars. After the incomprehensible time-span of 10^{16} years, these planet systems will have been destroyed as well. Over such a long time, all of the burned-out stars will collide with other star remnants and will tear the planets from their orbits. After 10^{19} years there won't be any galaxies either — they will have lost more and more star remnants into space. Other parts of the galaxies will be drawn into the huge, central black holes and only a few white dwarves, neutron stars, smaller black holes, and some gases, dust, and radiation will remain.

Is the Universe Infinite?

How did earlier cultures picture the universe?

People have been systematically observing the skies for thousands of years now. Early astronomers had practical reasons for the work they did. They wanted to help sailors navigate better and to make accurate calendars. They also wanted to understand the will of the gods. For these early stargazers astronomy — scientific study of the stars — and astrology — reading the future in the stars — were inseparable. Cosmology, too, is very old and is not something we developed in the last hundred years. Cosmology is the study of the ordering and history of the universe. The philosophers and astronomers in ancient Greece were especially interested in studying and explaining the universe. Except for a few outsiders, these philosophers and astronomers believed the Earth was the center of the universe. The earliest theories saw the Earth as a disk floating on a huge ocean. By about 600 BC, however, most thinkers had recognized that the Earth is shaped like a ball.

In the course of the next hundred years — during the 6th century BC — the ancient Greeks finally proved that the Earth was a globe. In the year 220 BC, the Greek scholar Eratosthenes even calculated the circumference of the Earth — the distance around the Equator — as 250,000 stadia. We aren't sure how long a "stadium" (plural "stadia") was, but most es-

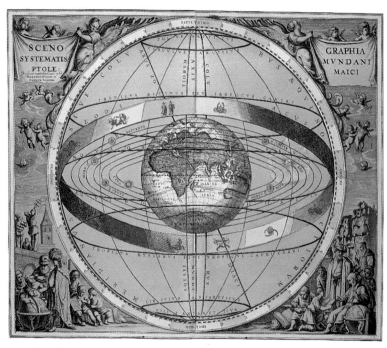

A model of the universe as it was imagined before Copernicus' time. Even after Copernicus many people still believed that the Earth was at the center of the universe and that the universe had a boundary — the sphere that held the fixed stars.

timates suggest this was somewhere between 24,000 and 28,000 miles. In any case he was less than 15% off the actual measurement: 24,902 miles. But he, too, thought the Earth was the center of the universe. Earth was "nested" in a series of larger and larger crystalline spheres, to which the planets, the Moon, and the Sun were attached. The entire universe was enclosed in an outermost sphere, to which the constellations were fixed. Until about 450 years ago, most people still believed that this starry shell was the end of the universe, and that beyond it only the gods existed, if anything. Humans couldn't see the realm of the gods, however, so the visible world had a clear boundary

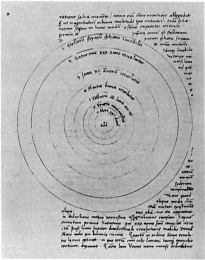

Nicolaus Copernicus placed the Sun at the center of the universe. He correctly recognized that the Earth is orbiting the Sun and that it also revolves on its axis. He still believed, however, that the universe was bounded by a sphere to which the stars were attached.

for them. Even Copernicus still believed the stars were attached to a sphere enclosing the universe.

What was the "Copernican Revolution"?

In 1501, the great Polish astronomer Nicolaus Copernicus (1473 – 1543) published a small book in which he cautiously suggested that the Sun might be at the center of the universe. His book "On the Revolutions of the Celestial Spheres," which was published the year he died, finally removed the Earth from its throne at the center of all creation and replaced it with the Sun. Previously people believed that all the universe revolved around the Earth. Copernicus showed that it is we who are rotating, not the universe. This important change in our view of the universe became known as the "Copernican Revolution."

Copernicus wasn't the first to suggest the Earth orbited the Sun, however. In the year 265 BC the Greek astronomer Aristarchus made the same claim. Neither of them was able to prove this theory scientifically though. This was left to future astronomers. The Italian physicist Galileo Galilei was the first astronomer to use a telescope to observe the stars. He was able to show that the planet Venus sometimes looked like a crescent moon and sometimes like a full moon. This only makes sense if the Earth is moving — orbiting the Sun together with the other planets.

Why does it get dark at night?

About 200 years ago, the German astronomer Heinrich Olbers (1758 – 1840) believed he had found proof that the universe was not infinite — the fact that it gets dark at night. If

If you stand in a small forest, you can see between the tree trunks to the space beyond. In an "infinitely" large forest, however, all the openings are blocked by tree trunks. Likewise, in an infinitely large universe there wouldn't be any gaps between stars. Some would be much further away than others would, but at every point in the sky there would have to be a star.

the universe were infinitely large, he argued, then no matter where you looked in space, there would have to be a star. In a very large forest, no matter which way you look, your view is blocked by a tree. If the universe were infinite, this would be true of stars as well: wherever you looked in the sky you would see a star. If there were stars in every direction, however, there couldn't be any dark spaces between them — in thick forest you can't see the sky beyond the trees. The entire sky would be a bright wall of fire! Night would be just as bright as day. Since it gets dark at night, Olbers said, there can't be an infinite number of stars. There must be a boundary beyond which there are at least no more stars.

Of course, some people objected to "Olbers' Paradox." They said that clouds of dust might be hiding distant stars. But an infinite number of stars, shining since the beginning of time, would long ago have burned away such clouds. Could it be that there really is a boundary to the universe, something first suggested by the ancient Greeks?

> **What was astronomy like at the beginning of the 20th century?**

Even in the early 20th century astronomers still believed that the limits of the Milky Way were the limits of the universe, or at least of the stars. There was empty space beyond our galaxy, but no more star systems. This made it easy to explain the dark night sky. Even though our galaxy is big, it isn't nearly big enough for there to be a star in every direction you look. There are many dark spaces between stars. Only along the Milky Way, where the concentration of stars is very high, is the night sky fairly bright.

If you look up from the plane of the Milky Way instead of along it, the sky is darker — but you can see star clusters that surround our galaxy. You can also see spiral nebulas, which we now know are actually distant galaxies. In the early 20th century, astronomers thought the spiral nebulae were large spiraling clouds of gas and that they belonged to our galaxy.

If we look away from the disk of the Milky Way out into deep space, we can see lots of spiral nebulae. People used to think that they were clouds of gas — nebula is the Latin word for "mist" — but we now know they are distant galaxies.

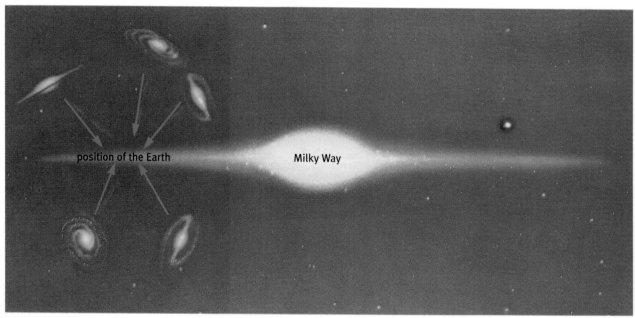

position of the Earth   Milky Way

The Andromeda Galaxy consists of gas, dust, a lot of dark matter, and approximately 400 billion stars. It is about 3 million light years away.

GALACTIC DISTANCES

are hard to measure. Astronomers look for a "reference star" in the galaxy they are observing – a star whose absolute, or real, brightness is known. They call such a star a "standard candle." The weaker the reference star appears, the further away the galaxy is. We once thought the Andromeda galaxy was about 1 million light years away, then this figure was revised to 2.4 million, and recently the European satellite Hipparcos measured it at 3 million light years.

In the 1920's, the astronomer Edwin Hubble proved that the spiral nebulae are actually distant galaxies that are made up of billions of suns – as our own galaxy is. He also showed that these galaxies were much further away than any of the star clusters previously discovered. The Andromeda nebula is three million light years away from us. Light from its stars takes three million years to reach us. Many of the stars that we can now see in this galaxy actually burned out a long time ago, and if one exploded today, it would take three million years before the news reached us! Hubble had opened the door to the world of multiple galaxies. The question of the limits of the universe had to be raised all over again.

In the three decades following Hubble's discovery, astronomers found more and more galaxies. Soon, the number of galaxies discovered had reached millions! The further away from us they were, the faster they seemed to be moving away from us. The realm of the galaxies – and therefore the universe, too – seemed to be without boundaries. But why, then, was the night sky dark? If Olbers was right and the sky had to be a bright wall of fire if the universe was infinite, then there had to be a boundary. A boundary like this seemed to contradict a principle that astronomers had seen confirmed again and again – the so-called "cosmological principle." It states that, in general, every region and every direction in space is more or less equal. No matter which direction astronomers in the 1950s looked, they always found similar conditions. Everywhere they found the same kind of stars and galaxies, and every comparable re-

Can the universe be finite and still have no boundaries?

A cluster of galaxies. In the part of the universe we can see, there are about 100 billion galaxies. Each galaxy often contains trillions of stars.

39

gion in space was like every other. A boundary, however, would contradict this principle, since a boundary is a special kind of place and not like everything else.

The conclusion astronomers reached was a very strange one: space must be without boundaries and yet finite as well. Is such a thing possible?

There are certainly surfaces that are finite and still have no boundaries. The surface of a ball or globe, for example, fits this description. If the Earth's surface were entirely covered with water a ship could sail in a straight line forever without reaching a boundary. If there are finite and yet unbounded surfaces (2 dimensions), then maybe there is also space (3 dimensions) with similar characteristics. Is space structured such that a fast spaceship could fly along a straight course and perhaps never reach a boundary — but would eventually return to its starting point? The universe would then be finite and yet have no boundaries. Of course, it is hard for us to imagine such a space, but that doesn't mean it can't exist.

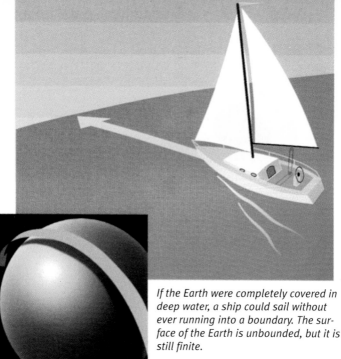

If the Earth were completely covered in deep water, a ship could sail without ever running into a boundary. The surface of the Earth is unbounded, but it is still finite.

front of the Sun and covers it completely, it is possible to see stars right next to the edge of the darkened Sun. Using very sensitive instruments, astronomers have shown that the light from these stars "bends" around the Sun, making it look like the star is in a different position than it normally is. This effect is very small, but we now know of many other examples of the deformation of space by

MODERN PHYSICS describes many things that we cannot see and that we cannot imagine. Nobody has ever seen an electron or a quark, even though they do exist. Deformed spaces and black holes probably exist, too, even though we can't imagine what they might look like.

What is space deformation?

The great physicist Albert Einstein (1879 – 1955) and his followers demonstrated that huge masses could deform space. Rays of light travelling through this space would appear to bend. Even the Sun has enough mass to bend light. This can be proven during a total eclipse of the Sun. When the Moon passes in

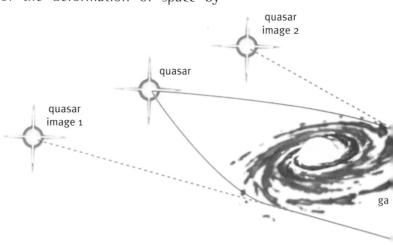

Large masses deform or "bend" space. If a galaxy with a tremendous mass lies between the Earth and a quasar, the galaxy deforms the space nearby and also deforms the quasar's light rays moving through this space. We then see 2 or more images of a single quasar.

huge masses. The light given off by distant quasars – galaxies in their early stages – is sometimes bent so much by galaxies between the quasar and the Earth that it passes around both sides of the

The Hubble Space Telescope has identified many gravitational lenses and has shown how space is warped by large masses. Here we see multiple images of the same object.

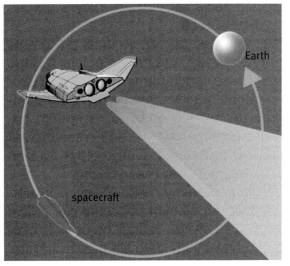

Is the universe un-bounded and yet finite? Would a spacecraft flying continuously in a straight line return to its starting point one day?

Earth

spacecraft

galaxy. We then see double or multiple images of the same quasar. The light bends as if it were passing through a lens – in fact, this phenomenon is called a "gravitational lens."

It is quite possible that the whole universe is bent like this. What seems to us to be a flat plane could actually be something like the surface of a ball. The universe would then be without boundaries but still finite – or, as astrophysicists put it, "closed." To determine whether or not the universe is really finite, we would have to know the average density of mass in the universe. If the average density is high it would deform space such that it is finite. This is only possible once a certain critical density

has been reached, however. This "critical density" or "closure density" is precisely the density required to collapse the expanding universe.

There probably isn't enough mass in the universe to make space finite, however. But if it is infinite or at least unimaginably large, then once again, at every point in the sky there should be a bright star from some distant galaxy. The whole sky would have to be one bright expanse. Once again we are faced with an apparent contradiction.

The solution to this problem lies in the fact that space is not infinitely old. It came into being about 15 billion years ago and has been expanding ever since.

Can we see to infinity?

The inflation theory, mentioned above, states that the universe expanded extremely rapidly after the big bang. If this is correct, then the tiny bubble of space that was the newborn

Earth

universe is now inconceivably large. Astronomers calculate that it would have a radius of $10^{2,000}$ light years. That's a one with 2,000 zeroes! We can only see a tiny part of this gigantic space — the universe is only 15 billion years old, after all, and the light from a galaxy 100 billion light years away hasn't had enough time to reach us yet.

The deeper into space we look, the further back into history we are seeing. When we see even our own Sun, we are seeing it as it was about 8 minutes ago — since its light takes that long to reach us. When we look at the star Vega we see it as it was 25 years ago. We see the star Deneb as it was 2,000 years ago and the Andromeda galaxy as it was about 3 million years ago. We see even more distant galaxies as they were hundreds of millions of years ago. This is how long the light has taken to reach us. Of course, the opposite is also true. Even if the inhabitants

of these distant galaxies had adequate telescopes, they would only be able to see dinosaurs roaming the Earth. There is no way they could know about humans. The "message" that we exist on Earth couldn't have reached them yet.

Astronomers who study quasars see them as they were billions of years ago. Inhabitants of such distant galaxies couldn't possibly know the Earth exists. News of its creation can't have reached them, since it can only travel at the speed of light. Even if extraterrestrial beings do exist, it is hardly likely that they would have the technological means of finding one small planet in such a distant galaxy.

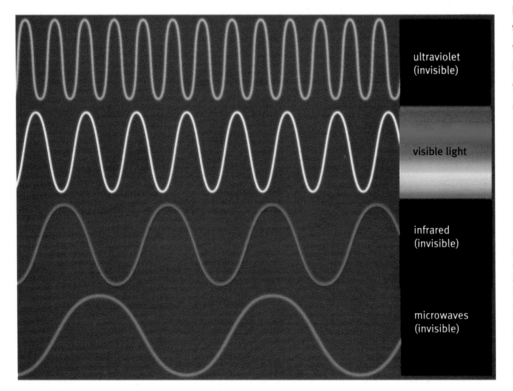

The wavelength of the light that was emitted by the hot, primal gas billions of years ago has become longer and longer because of expansion of the universe, and this "light" reaches us as invisible but measurable microwave radiation.

WAVES AND QUANTA

Light and similar phenomena, like ultraviolet and infrared rays, are usually described as waves. There are, however, experiments showing that light behaves more like a stream of particles than a wave. These particles are called light quanta, or "photons." Light, even if we cannot imagine it, behaves both like a particle and like a wave. This kind of behavior is also referred to as "dualism."

ultraviolet (invisible)

visible light

infrared (invisible)

microwaves (invisible)

The spectrum of electromagnetic waves reaches from the longest radio waves to the shortest waves of cosmic radiation. This illustration shows the sequence of invisible ultraviolet radiation, visible light, and then infrared and microwave radiation, both also invisible. "Cosmic background radiation consists of microwaves.

| 15 billion years | 7 billion years | 3 billion years | 300,000 years | 0 years |

gas prior to the formation of quasars and galaxies

non-transparent horizon in deep space

quasars

galaxies

A glimpse into the depths and the past of space. At the "horizon" we see the universe as it was shortly after the big bang.

QUANTUM ENERGY

The shorter electromagnetic waves are, the more energy their quanta have. X-rays have a shorter wavelength than visible light and their quanta therefore have much more energy. Light quanta move at the speed of light. This speed is not possible for an electron or a proton because, according to Einstein, its mass would then be infinitely big.

But, if we really are seeing further into the past the deeper we look into space, then at some point we would have to find a region beyond the galaxies and quasars where it would look to us like the universe had just been born. We should be able to see what the universe was like just after the big bang!

As we mentioned before, the universe was opaque right after the big bang. After about 300,000 years, however, it became transparent. At this point it was made up of — among other things — gases at temperatures around 5,400 °F. In other words, beyond the galaxies and quasars we should be able to see a white-hot wall of gas, far

beyond the distant quasars. The night sky ought to be bright, since we should see this gaseous wall of fire in every direction we look.

Since this bright light first began its journey, however, the universe has expanded immensely. At the same time the wavelength of these first rays has been stretched. The bright light emitted by the hot gas does reach us, but it reaches us as microwaves. Our eyes can't see this radiation, but we can pick it up with the right kind of antennas. This "background radiation" is considered evidence that the big bang theory is correct.

The furthest thing we can perceive is thus the hot primal gas that made up the newborn universe. We can't see any further back in time than the beginning. The hot gas thus surrounds us like a horizon and we can't see beyond it. This horizon is dark, and it seems to send out invisible microwave radiation. It is of course very far away, but not so far that there has to be a star in any direction we look. Between the stars and galaxies there are plenty of gaps through which we can see the pitch black horizon.

Even if the universe is infinite or immeasurably large, we can only see a small part of it. There isn't really a boundary, however, but only a "horizon" that we can't see beyond.

Extraterrestrial Life

Is there life on other planets in our solar system?

Given what we know about the universe, we can assume that there are billions of solar systems with Earth-like planets. It is very unlikely we will ever reach these planets in spaceships, however. With the technology we have today, however, it is comparatively easy to explore the Earth's immediate neighbors like the Moon, Venus, and Mars. It is certainly possible that space probes might one day discover life on a neighboring planet.

Although the planet closest to the Sun — Mercury — and the planets most distant from it — like Jupiter and Saturn — were probably never inhabited, it is certainly conceivable that there was once life on Mars or Venus. The average temperature on Venus is probably about 900 °F, however, and the planet is therefore uninhabitable in its present state. The situation on Mars is less clear. As recently as the beginning of the 20th century, people were firmly convinced that there were intelligent beings living on Mars. The Italian astronomer Schiaparelli believed he had dis-covered a canal system on Mars, and he thought this was proof of a highly advanced civilization. We have since learned that there are no such canals on Mars. Even pyramid-shaped formations and a mountain that looks something like a human face are no proof that there was once an advanced civilization on Mars. These could easily have been created by natural forces. Even here on Earth there are many examples of large blocks of stone that look like sculptures created by human artists.

Two space probes — Viking 1 and Viking 2 — landed on Mars in 1976, but were unable to find any evidence of life there. The planet does have an atmosphere, but it is so thin that it does not block dangerous radiation from the Sun. The surface of Mars also has no water where life-forms could find protection from this radiation. It takes a certain atmospheric pres-

Is the "Venus Man" just a group of lava flows?

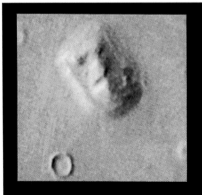 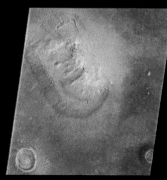 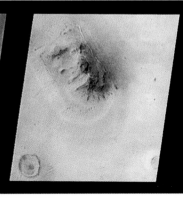

The "Face on Mars." It looks like it was made by Martians, but it is actually a naturally formed mountain as these photos taken by "Mars Global Surveyor" show.

A hundred years ago some people believed that there was an advanced civilization on Mars and that Martians had built a massive canal system. The canals turned out to be optical illusions.

A JOURNEY TO MARS would be conceivable using current technology. A manned spaceship would take 10 months to get there. After a stay of around 16 months, the return journey would last around 9 months. It will probably be many years before there is a manned mission to Mars, however. Still, people and materials are already being prepared for this exciting event. Russian cosmonauts have proven that human beings can cope with long stays in space quite well.

sure for water to be able to collect on the surface in liquid form, and Mars' atmosphere is too light for this. But was Mars always like this?

Satellite pictures show huge, dried up riverbeds in several different places. There must have been water flowing here at one time. Mars probably once had a denser atmosphere, allowing rivers and oceans to form. It is quite possible that there were once simple life forms on Mars. Many scientists think it was probably a collision with a planetoid that caused Mars to lose almost its entire atmosphere. There are other theories that try to explain why Mars is dry and inhospitable. The tremendous amounts of new information gathered by the "Mars Global Surveyor" and "Mars Pathfinder" probes will certainly lead to a much better understanding of the "Red Planet." In 1996 scientists at NASA also announced that they had examined a meteor they believe came from Mars, and that it showed evidence indicating that simple life forms may once have existed on Mars. These life-forms weren't little green men, however, but very tiny organisms. A Mars probe scheduled for launch in 2001 will gather rock samples in an attempt to find fossil evidence of ancient life on Mars.

Are there other planetary systems?

Every once in a while we see articles in the newspaper announcing that astronomers have discovered planets orbiting distant suns. These planets can't be observed through a telescope, however. When seen from far-away Earth, these planets are very close to their suns and are obscured by their light. It is possible to view distant planets indirectly, however. All planets exert a small amount of gravitational force on their central suns. This force pulls the suns a little bit off of their otherwise straight courses. In other cases this force makes the central star move slightly toward

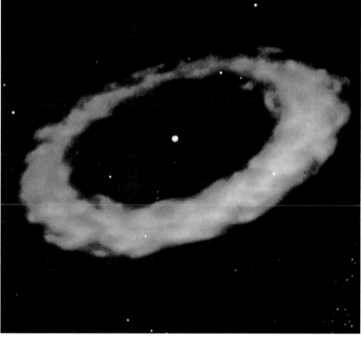

Infrared telescopes discovered disks of dust long before the Hubble Space Telescope was finished. Planets could form from a disk like this.

us and then away from us again. This makes the star look like it is wobbling, and very sensitive instruments can pick up this movement. Many measurements like this lead scientists to conclude that some of our neighboring suns also have planets orbiting them.

This really shouldn't surprise us, if we consider that the same kinds of matter exist throughout the universe and the same natural laws according to which stars and planetary systems are formed. There is also the data returned by the Hubble Space Telescope and several satellites that have shown large disks surrounding young stars. These disks will probably form planetary systems – as the disk around our young Sun did. There is no reason to believe that this hasn't already happened many times throughout the universe.

Huge radio telescopes are often used to try to receive signals from extraterrestrial civilizations.

Even though no one has yet been able to prove that life exists on other planets, there are good reasons for believing there might be other inhabited planets in the universe. It is generally true that nothing is unique in the universe. The same types of

Are we really alone in space?

galaxies, the same types of stars, and the same elements can be found everywhere in the universe. So why couldn't life also evolve elsewhere? We may not yet have any evidence for this, but we know that the universe is full of the same complex organic molecules that are the basis of life. These compounds have been discovered in meteorites and in areas of space where new stars form.

In 1985 the US space probe "Pioneer 10" left our solar system. In a few hundred thousand years this probe might travel past a star with inhabited planets. If this unlikely situation ever arises, the probe has a plaque containing information about the Earth and its inhabitants.

How can we make contact with extra-terrestrials?

The Voyager probes, which have already successfully visited the outer planets of our solar system – Jupiter and Saturn, for example – will also leave our solar system forever. They also contain information, stored on a videodisk, for the extraterrestrials who may someday find the probes. The disk contains pictures of the Earth, greetings, and recordings of music. 100,000 years from now this might be the final monument to our culture! With the help of a player included on the probes, it is theoretically possible that somewhere in the universe intelligent beings will hear the works of Bach and Mozart – millions of years from now. But if extraterrestrials do exist, will they get our message and reply while the Earth still exists?

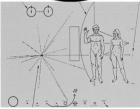

A "message in a bottle" for extraterrestrial civilizations. Above, the plaque attached to the Pioneer probe, and above it, the videodisk sent with the Voyager probes.

UNIMAGINABLE DISTANCES between Earth and even the nearest stars make it unlikely that we will ever hear from other intelligent beings in the universe. The space probe Voyager 2, for example, will have passed thirteen suns by the year 958,000 – the first one probably after 70,000 years. Voyager 2 won't pass Sirius, the brightest star we can see on Earth, until the year 290,000. Even if one of the planets belonging to these stars were inhabited, and the extraterrestrials living there received our message and also understood and answered it, it is highly unlikely that there would still be humans to receive the answer.

UFOs

Again and again we hear reports about Unknown Flying Objects or "UFOs." Are they extraterrestrial spaceships? Many UFO sightings can be easily explained. Satellites, unusually bright planets, weather balloons, certain cloud formations, and even disco lights can be mistaken for alien spaceships. We are still left with a small percentage of UFOs that cannot be explained. For most researchers, however, this still isn't enough to prove the existence of extraterrestrial life.

Even if there are Earth-like planets nearby, the chances that they are at the same stage of development are very small. On one there might still be dinosaurs running around, on another everything may be dead or in ruins.

There are much faster messengers into outer space than probes with plaques and disks, however: light and radio waves. Many researchers have tried searching for messages from space using very large radio telescopes. Some have also been sending contact messages into space. A cosmic telephone call with the inhabitants of a planet only five light years away would still be possible within the lifetime of a researcher: the answer to the question "Hello, is there anybody out there?" would be back here after 10 years!

Systematic searches for extraterrestrials are still going on. Astronomers are searching for and studying stars that might have inhabitable planets. The largest of these projects is called SETI (Search for Extraterrestrial Intelligence). So far, however, these projects have not found any evidence of extraterrestrial life.

Why haven't we heard from extraterrestrials?

Under the best of circumstances, radio telescopes can receive signals sent from 80 to 100 light years away. Even if there are one or two planets in this range that support intelligent life, the chances are slim that they have the technology to send such messages or receive them. The life on these planets may not have evolved intelligent beings yet. Perhaps there are only dinosaurs there, creatures who need another hundred million years of evolution before they can read our messages. It is also possible that the intelligent life in these distant systems died out long ago. The next planet with inhabitants that could send us messages is probably so far away that their radio signals would be too weak for our instruments to hear

Index

A

Andromeda galaxy/nebula 17, 19, 39, 42
antimatter 26
asteroids 22
atomic nuclei
  formation of 26, 27
  heavy 27, 28
  light 8, 26
atoms
  anatomy of 23, 24
  formation of 26-28

B

background radiation 32
big bang 7, 24-27, 32-34
binary star 14, 18
Big Dipper 32
black holes
  formation of 12, 13
  galactic 16, 17, 28, 34
brown dwarf 10, 17

C

carbon 11, 29
constellations 7
Copernican Revolution 37
Copernicus, Nicolaus 37

D

dark matter 15-17, 28, 33-34
Doppler effect 20

E

Earth
  formation of 16, 30, 31
Einstein, Albert 33, 34, 40
electrons 23-27
elementary particles 24, 26
extraterrestrial life 44-47

F

fixed stars 10, 36, 38
fundamental forces 24-26

G

galaxies
  clusters 18, 19, 28
  formation of 27-29
  types of 17, 18

Galilei, Galileo 4, 37
globular star cluster 14, 15, 23, 28

H

halo 15
Hawking, Stephen 14
helium 7, 8, 11, 27, 28, 30, 32
Hubble, Edwin 20, 39
Hubble Space Telescope 1, 5, 17, 20
hydrogen 7, 8, 11, 22, 27-30

I

inflation 24, 26, 41
iron 22, 27-30

L

light
  speed of 8
  quanta 42, 43
  waves 42, 43
Local Group 18

M

Magellanic Clouds 17, 18
Mars 22, 44, 45
matter 10, 12, 16, 23, 26-31
Mercury 11, 44
meteorites 21, 22, 30, 31, 46
Milky Way 15-18, 23, 28, 29, 38
molecules 28, 31, 32, 46
Moon 4, 5, 9, 18, 25, 36, 40, 44

N

neutrinos 6, 17, 26, 35
neutron star 11, 28, 35
neutrons 12, 23-28
nuclear fusion 7, 10, 11, 17
nucleons 27

O

oxygen 27-30

P

particle accelerator 7
particles (see elementary particles)
Planck, Max 33
planetoids 22, 32, 45
planets
  formation of pp. 10, 30

plasma 26
Pleiades 14
Pluto 16
powers of ten 24, 25
protons 23-28, 35
protostar 10
Proxima Centauri 9
pulsars 12

Q

quantum theory 33
quarks 23-26
quasars 17, 41, 42

R

radio waves 5, 8, 16, 42, 47
red giant 11
Relativity, Theory of 33

S

Saturn 30, 44, 46
Seven Sisters, The (see Pleiades)
singularity 24
solar system 22, 23, 29, 30
solar mass 12
space 33
  deformation of 40, 41
standard candle 23, 39
stars
  death of 11
  formation of 9
  maps 15
Sun death of 11
suns (see stars)
supernovas 11, 21, 29

T

telescopes types of 4-6

U

UFOs 47

V

Venus 44

W

white dwarf 11, 12, 35